Now I Know

Look...
a Butterfly

Written by David Cutts

Illustrated by Eulala Conner

Troll Associates

Library of Congress Cataloging in Publication Data

Cutts, David.
   Look—a butterfly.

   (Now I know)
   Summary: Follows the development of a butterfly
from egg through caterpillar and cocoon to maturity.
   1. Butterflies—Juvenile literature.   [1. Butter-
flies]   I. Conner, Eulala, ill.   II. Title.
QL544.2.C87   595.78 '9   81-11369
ISBN 0-89375-662-8   AACR2
ISBN 0-89375-663-6 (pbk.)

10   9   8   7   6   5   4

Butterflies are beautiful.

There are many kinds of butterflies . . .

. . . of many different colors.

But when butterflies are young,
they look very different.

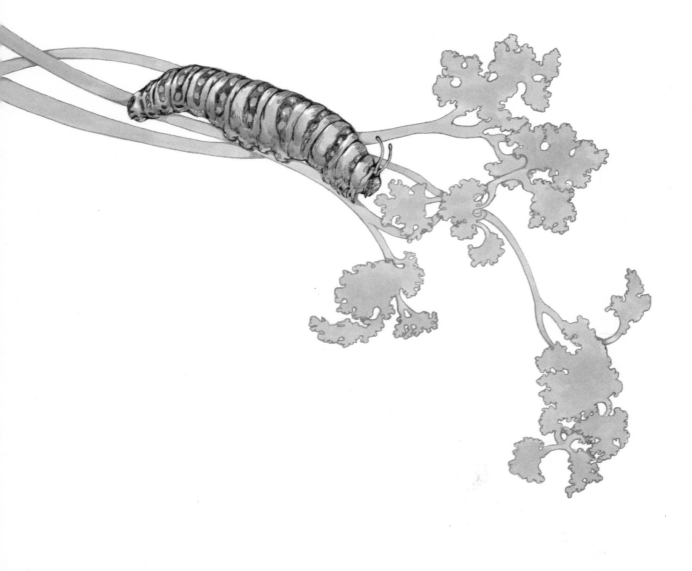

Butterflies lay eggs.
Inside, something is growing.

Caterpillars crawl out of the eggs.

The caterpillars start eating leaves.

Some caterpillars are smooth.

And some are bumpy or hairy.

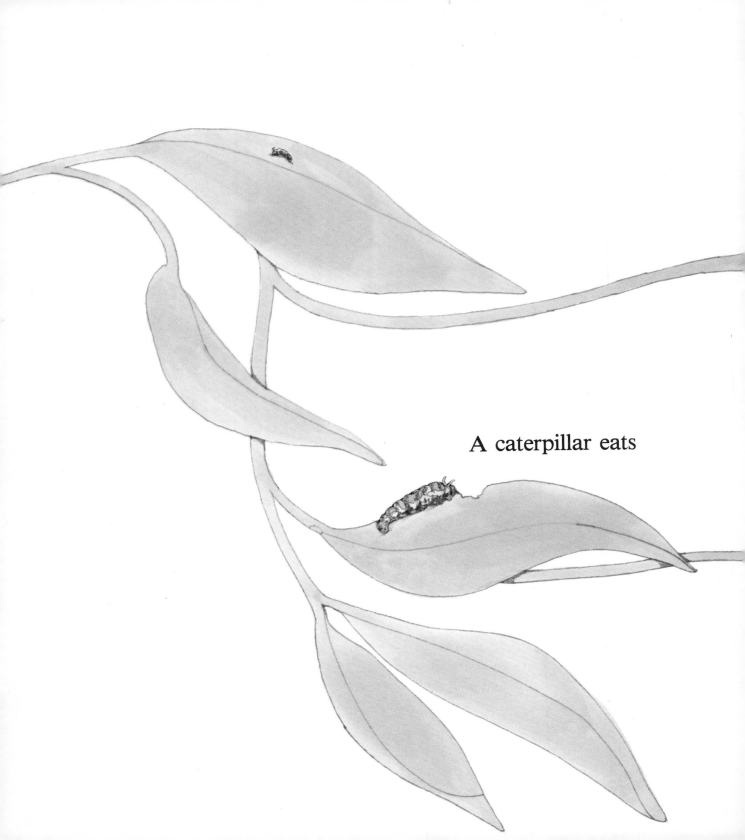

A caterpillar eats

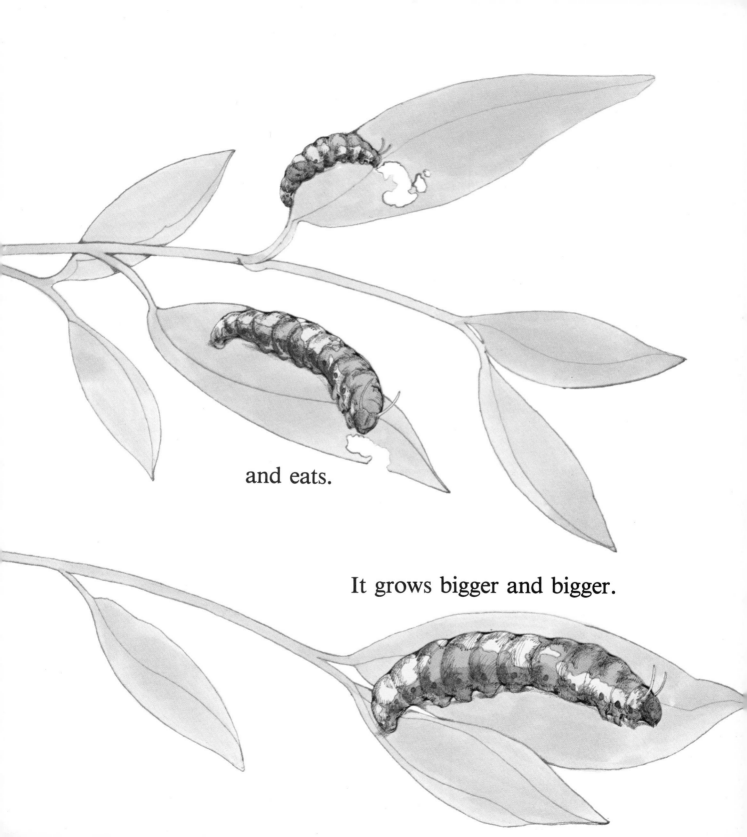

and eats.

It grows bigger and bigger.

At last, the caterpillar stops eating.

Its skin starts to come off!

A hard shell starts to form.

Inside the shell, the caterpillar
is becoming a butterfly.

Crack! Now what is happening?

Something is coming out of the shell.

It is a butterfly!

After a while the butterfly spreads its wings
and flies away.

This is a monarch butterfly.
It is orange and black.

This is a swallowtail butterfly.
It is brown and yellow.

This is a sulphur butterfly . . .

and this is a cabbage butterfly.

Butterflies love flowers.
They get their food from flowers.

All day long, butterflies go from flower to flower.
It's fun to watch them fly.

And if you see a funny caterpillar crawling, remember . . .

someday, it may become a beautiful butterfly!